Thank you for your purchase, to show my appreciation:
https://chelseak532002550.wordpress.com/books-for-sharing/

© 2021 Chelsea Kong

All rights reserved. All images used in this book are licensed copies from their respectful owners. This book or any portion thereof may not be reproduced or used in any manner
whatsoever without the express written permission of the publisher except for the use of brief quotations in a book review.

Printed in 2021, Made in Toronto, Canada
ISBN: 978-1-7775796-4-7
Library and Archives Canada

The Lord grant you the desires of your heart.

Surely the Lord GOD will do nothing, but he reveals his secret unto his servants the prophets (Amos 3:7).

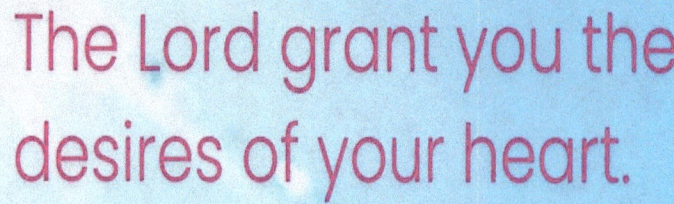

Dreams are important for us.

God gives us visions and dreams.

We need to dream daily.

It is a group of images, thoughts, or emotions in our minds when we sleep.

God can use dreams to speak to us to warn us.

DREAMS OF GOD'S PROMISE

God used a vision to remind Abraham about His promise for a son (Genesis 15:1).

Jacob had a dream of a ladder reaching to heaven with angels going up and down. He got God's promise of Abraham's blessings will come through him.
(Genesis 28:10-17).

WARNING DREAMS

They can be scary.

Pharoah's Dreams about the famine (Genesis 41:1-7).

Joseph was told to leave Bethlehem because King Herod wanted to kill Jesus (Matthew 2:13).

Abimelech was warned not to touch Sarah (Genesis 20:1-7).

DREAMS ABOUT THE FUTURE

Joseph before he became prime minister (Genesis 37:1-11).

The Cupbearer and the Baker (Genesis 40-41).

Samuel about judgment (1 Samuel 3).

The Midianite and Amalekite armies (Judges 7:12-15)

King Nebuchadnezzar had dreams (Daniel 2,4).

Solomon had a dream that God asked what He wants (1 Kings 3:5).

Daniel had dreams about the future.

Joseph had a dream about Jesus (Matthew 1:20).

KNOW WHAT THE DREAMS MEAN

And he said, Hear now my words: If there be a prophet among you, [I] the LORD will make myself known unto him in a vision, [and] will speak unto him in a dream. (Numbers 12:6).

VISIONS OF GOD'S PROMISES

God gave Moses the instructions and picture of how the Tabernacle should look like (Exodus 25:1-9, 31:1-11, 40:33-38, Hebrews 9:1-7).

Zacharias had a vision about John (Luke 1:5-23).

God gave Paul a vision of heaven (2 Corinthians 12:1-6).

God may show you a place you will go.

Peter had a vision before he visited Cornelius (Acts 10:9-15).

John sees visions of the future (Revelation).

There are different kinds of dreams.

We can also get ideas from God in our dreams.

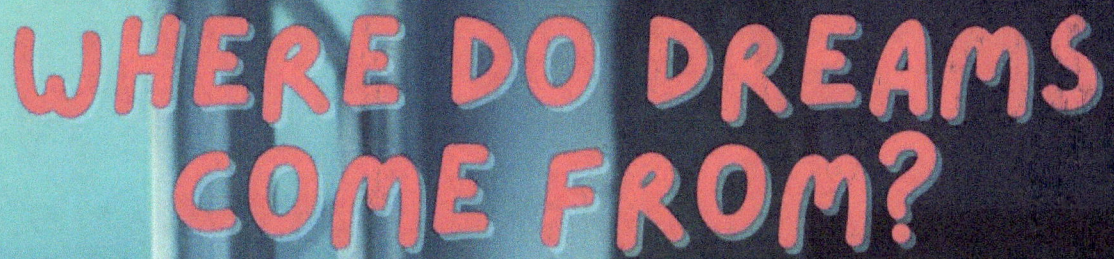

WHERE DO DREAMS COME FROM?

God

You

The Evil One.

BAD DREAMS

The evil one can give us bad dreams.

We need to pray to stop the bad dreams from happening.

Ask God why you had the dream and what it means.

Change it by doing what God tells us.

BAD DREAMS

The evil one can give us bad dreams.

We need to pray to stop the
bad dreams from happening.

Ask God why you had the dream
and what it means.

Change it by doing what God tells us.

WRITE IT DOWN

Then the Lord replied: "Write down the revelation and make it plain on tablets so that a herald may run with it.

For the revelation awaits an appointed time; it speaks of the end and will not prove false. Though it linger, wait for it; it will certainly come and will not delay. (Habakkuk 2:2-3)

PRAY

A dream can change.

Ask God what the dream and vision mean.

Pray over it and do as God tells you.

A vision will happen and cannot be changed.

PRAY

Ask God how to change the dream and speak it out.

Speak the vision that God gives you.

What He tells you to write, speak it out loud.

SEE IT

See in your mind and daily.

See a clear picture of it.

You can draw it out.

ACT ON IT

1. Worship
2. Praise
3. Dance
4. Prayer
5. Give Thanks
6. Do whatever He tells you

DO IT EVERY DAY

Keep letting Holy Spirit bring you close to Him.

Talk to Him about your day.

Pray with Holy Spirit as much as you can.

Live each day knowing He is with you

SALVATION PRAYER

God, I know I sinned against you. Forgive me for the wrong that I have done. I believe that Jesus Christ died on the cross for me. That He rose from the grave so that after three days. I can have His long-lasting life. Come into my heart to be my Lord and Savior. I choose to turn away from my sins and I choose to follow you. Lead me to walk with you. Keep me safe and teach me your ways. Stop every bad thing in my life that has an open door to hurt me. Close those doors. Holy Spirit fill me now in Jesus' name. Amen.

BAPTISM IN THE HOLY SPIRIT

Jesus, you are the one that fills me with Your Spirit. Come Holy Spirit and come into my life and fill me to overflow with Your presence. Come with your fire too. Thank you for the gift of tongues in Jesus' name. Amen.

Open your mouth and let the words come out that God gives you. It will be words that you don't know what they mean. You can ask God what it means. You need to let Him talk through you every day to grow this gift.

He will bring you closer to God and you will know Jesus more. You will have power from God to do great things and know things.

🙏 PRAYER

Thank you, Father, for dreams and visions. I pray that you will give me the meaning to the dreams and visions that you give me. Teach me how to pray over them.

Guide my steps to walk in your ways and your plan safely in Jesus' name.
Amen.

Message from the Author

God speaks to us through dreams when He is not able to get us to hear Him when we are awake. Dreams can also give us ideas. Visions cannot be changed because God decides what He wants to do. We can also dream about heaven and hell. God brings people there so that they can share with others. He wants people to know Him. He wants them to have Jesus in their heart and the Holy Spirit to lead them. He wants us to put our trust in Him and tell Him everything. He will tell us what to do.

OTHER PRODUCTS

- Knowing God
- How to Hear God's Voice
- New Life in Jesus
- Loving Israel
- God's Gifts
- Meeting God
- Word Power
- Fruit of the Spirit
- The Tabernacle
- Bride for Jesus
- A Life of Prayer
- Live Free
- Who am I in Jesus
- Walk in Love
- God's Favor
- Man of God
- Woman of God
- How to Use Money
- God's Wisdom
- Fasting
- See Jerusalem and Bethany
- First Fruit Offering
- Feast of Trumpets
- Day of Atonement
- Feast of Tabernacles
- Counting the Omer
- Festival of Lights
- Glory, Presence, and Holy Spirit
- Live in God's Presence
- 31 Day Devotional
- Biblical Puzzle Book Vol 1
- Biblical Puzzle Book Vol 2
- Biblical Puzzle Book Vol 3
- Biblical Puzzle Book Vol 4
- Biblical Puzzle Book Vol 5
- Bible Puzzles for Young Children Book 1
- Bible Puzzles for Young Children Book 2
- Bible Puzzles for Young Children Book 3
- Biblical Puzzle for Children Books 1-3
- How God Speaks
- Knowing Jesus
- Knowing Holy Spirit

OTHER PRODUCTS

Teaching Series
How to Hear God's Voice Teaching Guide & Audio Book
Relationship with God, Jesus, Holy Spirit Guide
Knowing God, Jesus, Holy Spirit Guide & Audio Book

Teaching (Non-Sale)
Purim
Passover
Resurrection

More books to come!

More books on Amazon, Kobo, and Barnes and Noble
https://chelseak532002550.wordpress.com/

More books on Amazon, Kobo, and Barnes and Noble
https://www.amazon.com/author/chelseakong

Please leave a review to help the author continue to write more books to reach more readers. Thank you so much for your support.

About
CHELSEA KONG

She is a writer, creative arts and digital media artist, skilled administration professional, and podcaster. Chelsea also served in a variety of roles, from audiovisual, photography, to assisting on the worship team, and ministry team. She also has a passion for families being united.

Chelsea graduated from Hotel and Restaurant Management, Digital Media Arts, Office Administration, and experience working with children. She mainly writes children's books, stories, bridal writing, poems, lyrics for songs, words of encouragement, blessings, prayers, and jokes. The author of How to Hear the Voice of God, the Bridal Collection, Knowing God, etc. She also has her own Bible Puzzle books and other inspired products. Her podcast channel is called Chelsea K on Anchor, Spotify, and iTunes. She has been on Unity Live Radio and The Lady Tracey Show and is highly recommended by a Proud Christian blog.

Please check my website to find out more:
https://chelseak532002550.wordpress.com/